# Buffalo
# Shot Placement and Trophy Evaluation

# Buffalo
# Shot Placement and Trophy Evaluation

by

**KEVIN ROBERTSON**

Photos by

**CATHERINE ROBERTSON**

Artwork by

**SAMANTHA ROBERTSON & CATHY NEL**

Frontispiece by

**NATALIE ROBERTSON**

SAFARI PRESS ®

Robertson, Kevin
Robertson, Catherine

First edition

Safari Press Inc.
2009, Long Beach, California

ISBN 1-57157-335-6

Library of Congress Catalog Card Number: 2008927485

10 9 8 7 6 5 4 3 2 1

Printed in China

# OTHER BOOKS & DVDs by KEVIN ROBERTSON

## AFRICA'S MOST DANGEROUS
## The Southern Buffalo *(Syncerus caffer caffer)*

It was Kevin Robertson who came up with the idea of showing a "ghost view" of the vital organs on African big game, and his books have sold tens of thousands of copies. His latest book in the series is the most comprehensive guide to shot placement for the African buffalo ever written, and it is our belief that no African hunter will want to be without this book.

He discusses his favorite calibers, what constitutes a good trophy, and when a buffalo should not be shot. He talks of hunting the cow buffalo, equally as dangerous as a bull, and he gives us his views and insights as to the suitability of the various rifle types and bullets. Many books on African hunting profess to deal with it all, but Robertson focuses on only one subject—the Cape or southern buffalo, the largest subspecies of buffalo and the one with the meanest and most ferocious reputation. This book includes information on the African tracker, bowhunting, caliber choices, choosing the right bullet, selecting rifle sights, trophy evaluation, anatomical features, differences between bulls and cows in the field, distribution and natural history, hunting accessories, and much more.

This lavishly produced book is illustrated with some of the most magnificent Cape buffalo photographs ever seen by world-class wildlife photographer Catherine Robertson. 2007 Long Beach, 243pp, color photos, 8.5x11, hardcover, dj. **Not Sold in Bookstores** ..........$59.95

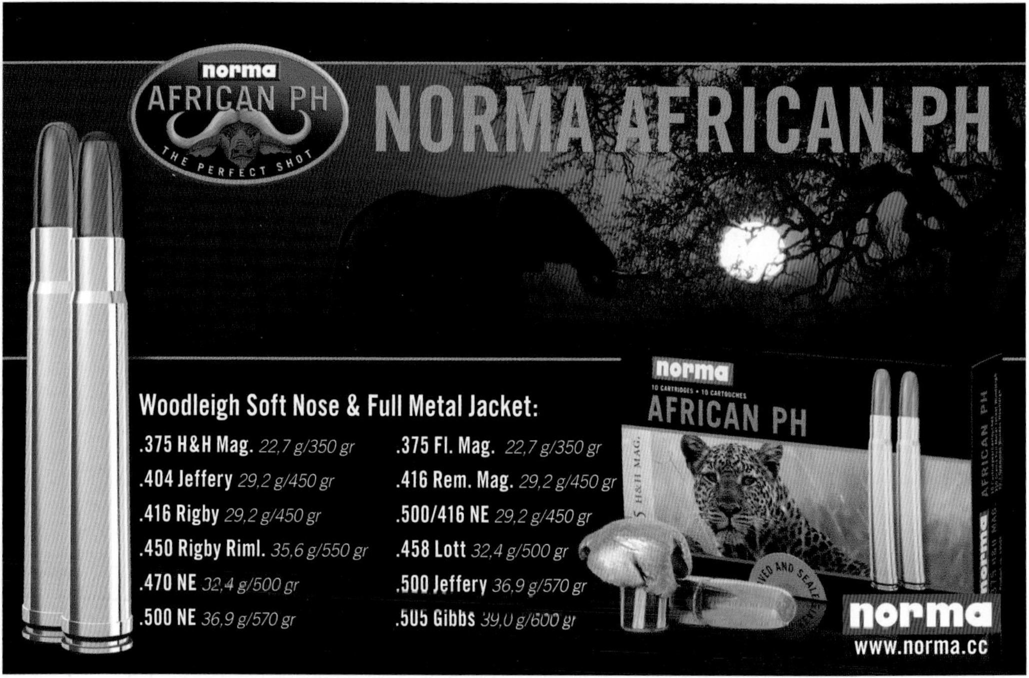
norma
AFRICAN PH
THE PERFECT SHOT
NORMA AFRICAN PH
Woodleigh Soft Nose & Full Metal Jacket:
.375 H&H Mag. 22,7 g/350 gr
.404 Jeffery 29,2 g/450 gr
.416 Rigby 29,2 g/450 gr
.450 Rigby Riml. 35,6 g/550 gr
.470 NE 32,4 g/500 gr
.500 NE 36,9 g/570 gr
.375 Fl. Mag. 22,7 g/350 gr
.416 Rem. Mag. 29,2 g/450 gr
.500/416 NE 29,2 g/450 gr
.458 Lott 32,4 g/500 gr
.500 Jeffery 36,9 g/570 gr
.505 Gibbs 39,0 g/600 gr
norma
10 CARTRIDGES • 10 CARTOUCHES
AFRICAN PH
norma
www.norma.cc

# OTHER BOOKS & DVDs by KEVIN ROBERTSON

Almost all varieties of African big game have very different "kill zones," but knowing where to place a killing shot is the most important criterion in hunting. Kevin Robertson, a PH and veterinarian, shows the anatomical features for all classes of African game—from elephant and buffalo to the large cats to the antelopes to the smallest game animals (duiker and warthog). Each animal is shown in a color field picture as well as a color "ghost view" that illustrates the shoulder bones, heart, lungs, and brain so that you will know precisely where to place your shot. 1999 Long Beach, 271pp, color photos, 8.5x11, hardcover, dj. .................................... **$65.00***

Available in DVD, running time 2 hours.... **$39.95**

Mini version.................................................. **$17.95**

***These books & DVD are Not Sold in Bookstores**

*This is the best bull buffalo it has been my privilege ever to have seen. With a spread of 50 inches, this approximately 13-year-old bull was a loner when Catherine photographed him. From his good body size, I expect him to have led a full and productive breeding life and with that, his genes would have been passed on. What awaits him now is a steady decline in his health and body condition as his teeth wear out. He'll either starve to death or become a victim of a lion attack. To me, he is absolutely the ideal trophy animal.*

*Happy Hunting!*

13 YEARS OLD

*"Scrum Caps" are old bulls that have lost both their horns, usually through fighting or as a result of being worn too thin from constant rubbing. Despite having no trophy value whatsoever, they are a challenge to hunt and popular with Continental sport hunters. This bull is at least 12 years old. Notice the hairless patches on his side, which are a sure sign of old age.*

*The life expectancy of buffalo bulls is thought to be about 15 years. From the look of this old fellow, I estimate him to be pretty close to this age. Old bulls like this are especially vulnerable to lion.*

## 13 OR 14 YEARS OLD

*It should be obvious that this is also an old bull of at least 13, maybe even 14 years. His horn spread will measure about 33 inches.*

*This grand old fellow is of a similar age. By now I hope it's easy to recognize that this is an old bull. To my way of thinking, this type of bull, with all that character about him, and that look of hate in his eyes, is by far the best type of buffalo to hunt as a trophy.*

**13 OR 14 YEARS OLD**

*This is what the horns of old 13- or 14-year-old bulls look like. Notice how blunt the tips are and how smooth many years of rubbing have made them. Old fellows like these have to have been super smart to have survived for so long, and therein lies the great challenge of sport hunting them.*

**12 YEARS OLD**

*With a spread of well over 40 inches and good curl, this* dagga *boy makes a fine trophy.*

*The hairless patches on this bull's face are typical for bulls of this age. A good, 45" spread; a solid boss; worn-down tips; and old age all contribute toward making him a most acceptable trophy.*

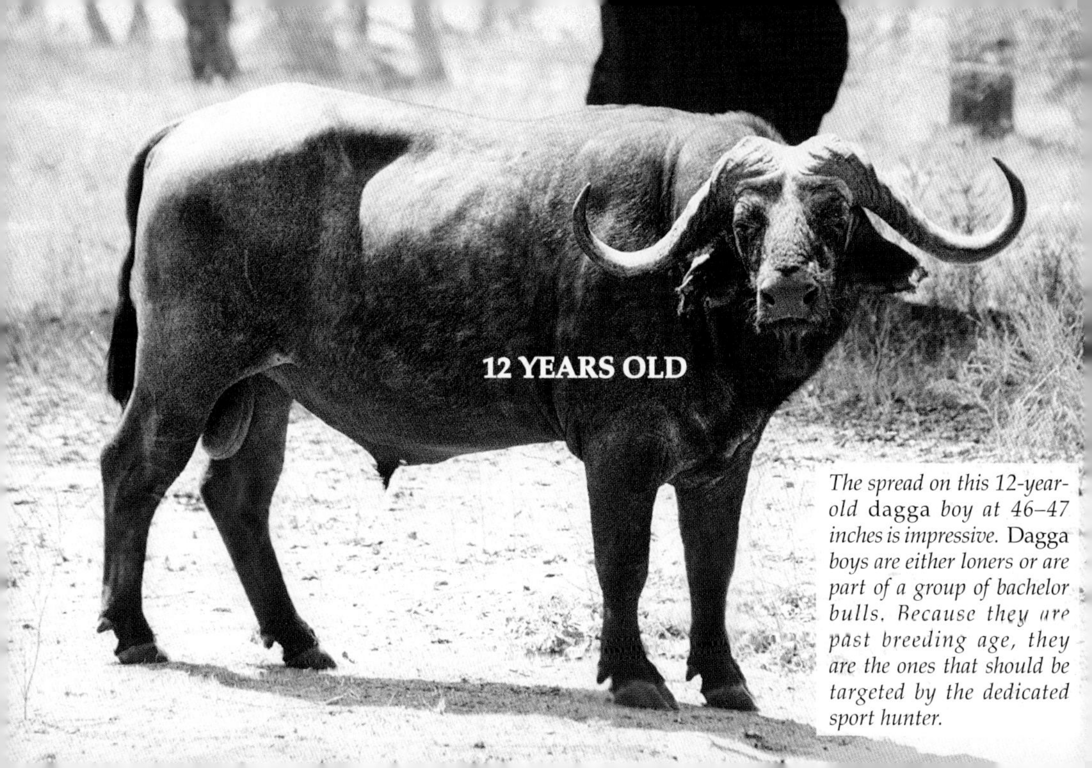


*The spread on this 12-year-old* dagga *boy at 46–47 inches is impressive.* Dagga *boys are either loners or are part of a group of bachelor bulls. Because they are past breeding age, they are the ones that should be targeted by the dedicated sport hunter.*

*The 12-year-old bull on the right has a truly magnificent boss and an almost 40-inch spread. Older bulls have already passed their genes on, and this is the type of buffalo trophy hunters should target. This old gentleman is a fine specimen and a worthy addition to any trophy room. That he will not make it into either of the record books should not be a consideration.*

*This impressive herd bull has a completely solid boss and well-worn horn tips. I estimate him to be late in his tenth or early in his eleventh year.*

## LATE 10 OR EARLY 11 YEARS OLD

*This massive bodied, thick-necked, and heavily shouldered buffalo was still a herd bull when photographed. He was a prime specimen of a dominant herd bull. Close observation will reveal bark on his horns from horn rubbing—a sure sign of a bull in a privileged, breeding social position.*

*This is typically what the horns and boss of a 10-year-old bull with a 40-inch spread looks like. Notice the white, hairless patches that are starting to develop on his face. They are a result of mite infestations and are associated with bulls that are this age and older.*

*This herd bull was in a disease-free buffalo-breeding program, which I worked with when I was still in Zimbabwe.*

## LATE 9 OR EARLY 10 YEARS OLD

*The massive boss is just about completely solid while the hugely muscular neck and pitch-black hide indicate that this bull is in his breeding prime. He is close to 40 inches. Notice the bark on his boss, which is from horn rubbing. This common, dominant bull activity changes the shape and shrinks the size of a bull's horns.*

*Here is another 9-year-old bull with horn tips still above his boss level. Despite this, the well-developed and easily visible ridges that are developing on his boss accurately put him at this age.*

*Despite the fact that this bull's horn tips are still high above the level of his boss, he is also in his ninth year. Notice also how much darker his neck and face are compared to the rest of his body; also note the well-muscled shoulders. These are the very obvious signs that he is an active breeding bull, pumped full of the male hormone testosterone. That his horn tips are still quite sharp puts him at this age.*

## 9 YEARS OLD

*I would place this bull with a 38-inch spread in the 9-year-old age group. Notice that his boss is just about completely solid, with only a small, soft, and puffy ridge remaining on the bottommost edge along the forehead. Notice also the dark-black coloring to the skin on his neck and on the bridge of his nose. This is a result of the male hormone testosterone, and it indicates that he is a prime breeding bull.*

*Be careful when the forehead of a buffalo is covered with mud as it can easily disguise the true extent of his boss development. Fairly blunt horn tips at boss level and careful observation should indicate that this 40-incher's boss is almost completely solid. This puts him in the at-least-9-year-old age bracket.*

## LATE 8 OR EARLY 9 YEARS OLD

*This buffalo was a herd bull when photographed as he grazed on the lush Lake Kariba shoreline. Close observation of his boss will show that it is just about, but not completely, solid in the mid-center area of his forehead. There is still a small, light-gray, triangular-shaped piece that is still soft and puffy. This fact ages this fine 45-incher as a late 8- or early 9-year-old bull.*

LATE 8 YEARS OLD

*Notice the boss is not completely solid in the middle of the forehead and the horn tips are still quite sharp. These factors age him quite accurately. The dark-black color of his body indicates that he is in his breeding prime.*

## LATE 8 YEARS OLD

*This bull with a 36-inch spread is well in his eighth year. On some bulls, the center of the boss will never become completely solid.*

*This bull's horn tips are high above the level of the boss, the top of his boss is hard, and the frontal center portion is not solid. These factors give a quite accurate estimate of age. Large variations in horn size and shape are a common and frustrating characteristic of the southern buffalo.*

*Even from a distance it should be obvious that this bull's boss is still not completely solid—even though he is a herd bull. The soft and puffy area on his forehead indicates he is only in his eighth year. Despite good curl and a spread of at least 40 inches, he is a breeder and should not be considered a trophy.*

*This is another photograph of the same 8-year-old bull. Notice his body shape and the degree of muscling to his shoulders and neck. He will soon be heavy enough to fight for dominance now that the top of his boss is also sufficiently hard. I estimate his companion (on right) to be of a similar age. Large variations to horn shape and size are one of the more frustrating characteristics of the southern buffalo subspecies.*

*The top of the boss is hard, but the triangularly shaped frontal center portion is not. This area still looks soft and puffy. Look at the position and level of his horn tips; note his shoulders, which are becoming deep and heavy. All these characteristics age him accurately to be in his eighth year. Despite a horn spread of about 40 inches, he is still too young to be considered a trophy.*

*Notice that the boss is hard and solid on the top on this 8-year-old, but that the lower edges on his forehead are not. His horn tips are still quite sharp and his curls are still above boss level. All these factors enable me to age him quite accurately. Photographed during a drought, he has lost body condition.*

**LATE 7 YEARS OLD**

*Horn tips of Addo buffalo from South Africa's Eastern Cape region characteristically remain high above the boss on 7-year-olds.*

*Despite being an exceptional buffalo, this bull is also still too young to be considered a trophy. It is evident that his boss is starting to develop, but it shows no sign of any hardness yet. This places him quite accurately into his $7^{th}$ year.*

*This bull was also in his seventh year when photographed. Notice his boss is covered in hair and "green." Notice also that his horn tips are still sharp and well above the level of the boss. Close observation of this bull over a three-day period revealed that he had the sexual desire to breed but could not because he had not yet attained the social ranking of a herd or breeding bull. Over this time I watched him being chased off repeatedly by older, solidly bossed herd bulls. While he is sufficiently heavy and well muscled, I estimated that it would take another year at least for his boss to develop sufficiently for him to be able to compete successfully for dominance and breeding favors. Unfortunately, I was never able to find this bull again.*

*How do we know this bull's age? His horn tips are still sharp and rearward pointing, and his boss, while formed, is still soft. Look also at his shoulders and neck to see how they are starting to muscle up. In another year he'll have bulked up enough to give him the weight and strength to fight successfully.*

**7 YEARS OLD**

*I estimate this bull to be in the middle of his seventh year. Notice how the top of his boss has become hard but the frontal center portion is still soft and hairy. Within the next six months his boss with change significantly and his tips will drop further. Notice also his dark-black body. This is another indication that his hormones are starting to bubble as he rapidly approaches prime breeding age.*

*Notice how the horn tips are dropping and the boss is starting to develop on this 7-year-old. These characteristics will change quickly within the next year or so.*

*The boss on this bull is still soft and hairy. The fact that he still has quite sharp, rearward pointing horn tips places him in his late sixth or early seventh year.*

*I estimate this young bull to be late in his sixth year. Please realize that there exists considerable variation to the amount of hair young buffalo bulls can have on their foreheads. This bull does not appear to have any.*

*The boss on this 6-year-old bull is still completely soft, hairy, and gray. Despite having good curl and close to a 40-inch spread, this bull is still too young to be considered a trophy.*

# 6 YEARS OLD

*This good view of a head of a buffalo from Addo National Park shows off his forehead clearly. It is evident that his boss is starting to develop, but it still has a long way to go before becoming hard. This fact, together with his still-sharp horn tips, places him as a 6-year-old.*

*Even though the horn tips on this young bull have dropped to below the level of his boss, the soft and still hairy nature of it indicate that he is only in his sixth year.*

**EARLY 6 YEARS OLD**

*This is the same young bull on page 106 a little more than a year later. I estimate him now to be early in his sixth year. Notice how his horns have changed and grown over this time. He will muscle-up and fill out, body-size-wise, as he matures. These are the secondary sexual characteristics associated with and influenced by the male hormone testosterone. Notice also how his boss is starting to grow and develop. Still hairy at this stage, it will require another two years at least before it will be hard enough for fighting. Most bulls attain sufficient body size and strength to fight successfully for breeding rights by their eighth year.*

# 4 YEARS OLD

*This young bull was in a disease-free buffalo-breeding program. Substantially better nutrition allows such buffalo to grow quicker and reach sexual maturity earlier. This in turn also affects their horn growth and development. Even at this stage it is obvious that this bull has little trophy potential.*

*This young bull is estimated to be late in his fourth year of life. Notice his look of "youth" and his long, sharp horn tips sticking up high above the level of his head.*

dominant breeding-bull behavior. This results in the tips of the horns being worn down and becoming blunt. Also, as the bull matures, the horn tips usually drop below the level of the boss. This has the effect of exposing the boss area for more effective head butting.

Here is a synopsis of the facts. Bulls reach sexual maturity at three to four years of age, but they only attain the body size, strength, experience, and the degree of boss development that enables them to compete for breeding rights by sometime in their eighth year. The life of a herd bull is stressful, and because of this they are usually only able to maintain this privileged position for two to three years. By late in their tenth or sometime in their eleventh year, herd or breeding bulls are usually replaced by younger, stronger, and fitter eight-year-old bulls. Life expectancy for bulls in a natural state is thought to be about fifteen years; most old bulls are killed and eaten by lion.

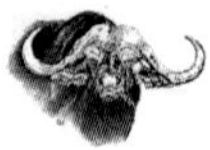

*Answer to question on page 103: The boss on this fine, 45-inch bull is just about completely solid. Because of this, I place him in the 9-year-old category. Because he is an active breeder, he is still too young to be considered a good trophy—despite his impressive spread and curl.*

## Buffalo: Shot Placement and Trophy Evaluation

The best visual method for determining the age of a male buffalo is to evaluate the degree of his boss development or "hardness." Horn characteristics like the length and sharpness of the horn tips and their position in relation to the forehead are also relevant. Secondary sexual characteristics like body size, degree of muscling in the neck and shoulder region, and a dark-black hide are all influenced by the male hormone testosterone. This is what gives bulls their sex drive and the aggression needed to fight for the right to breed. With experience, these characteristics become easily recognizable. They are also a useful aid in determining a bull's social ranking, breeding status, and age.

A bull buffalo develops a boss—the hard, bonelike horn that covers the top of the head—so that this area, and the brain which lies beneath it, is protected during violent test-of-strength contests. Only dominant herd bulls get to breed with receptive cows, and bulls need to fight for the right to become dominant. Such fights are test-of-strength, head-butting affairs, with the object of the exercise simply being to ascertain which bull is physically the strongest. Survival of the fittest/strongest is very much a part of nature, and in the grand scheme of things this results in only the biggest and strongest passing on their genes.

This is all part of the natural selection process, and for buffalo a solid boss is a perquisite. Contesting bulls do not try to kill each other at such times, simply because bulls are essential for the defense of the herd from lion. Horn rubbing, and consequently wear, is all part of

# Determining the Age of Bull Buffalo
## Chapter Eight

Buffalo reach sexual maturity when they attain approximately two-thirds (66 percent) of their genetically determined mature body weight. How quickly they attain this weight under natural conditions is totally dependent on the area, the climate, and the amount of rainfall. Rainfall patterns and, consequently, vegetation growth tend to be cyclical in nature. Because of this, there can be variations in buffalo growth rates from year to year, country to country, or even area to area within a country. Because of these factors, the age that an individual buffalo matures will differ.

The ages given in this publication are pretty accurate estimates for those buffalo from the Zambezi Valley because those are the ones with which I have had the most experience. Only careful dental analysis will reveal the exact age of a buffalo; it is impossible to determine an exact age from a photograph. Determining the age of a buffalo through visual appraisal only is not an exact science, but with experience, practice, and careful observation it is possible to be fairly accurate.

*Opposite page: Can you guess the age and horn size of this fine bull? See answer on page 105.*

*These are the same two bulls. On bulls with a spread of 40 inches or more, their horns will be wider than their rear end. See how the younger bull's spread is considerably wider than his backside.*

*Only from the front can horn spread and degree of boss development be assessed. The young, 7-year-old bull on the left has a spread of well over 40 inches. The 8-year-old bull on the right will have a spread of 35 to 36 inches.*

*Exceptional bulls with a spread of two hands width past the ear tips on each side will have a Rowland Ward measurement of 48 to 50 inches. Such bulls are few and far between.*

*This bull has a spread of 42 or 43 inches and is late 7 or early 8 years old.*

*Consider the human hand to be 4 inches wide, so this bull will measure 33″ + 4″ + 4″ = 41″. Using this method makes it easy to recognize bulls with spreads greater than 40 inches. I estimate this 8-year-old bull to have a spread of 42 inches.*

*A mature bull's straight line, tip-to-erect-ear-tip measurement is 32 to 33 inches. The spread on this 8-year-old breeding bull's horns must be close to 40 inches.*

## SCI MEASUREMENT

*SCI's measurement scoring system is very difficult to judge accurately in the field because it measures around the curves and includes the width of both bosses. Younger, soft-bossed bulls with good curl and long, sharp tips tend to score better than older bulls under this scoring system. An estimated straight-line, outside measurement on this 8-year-old herd bull is 35–36 inches.*

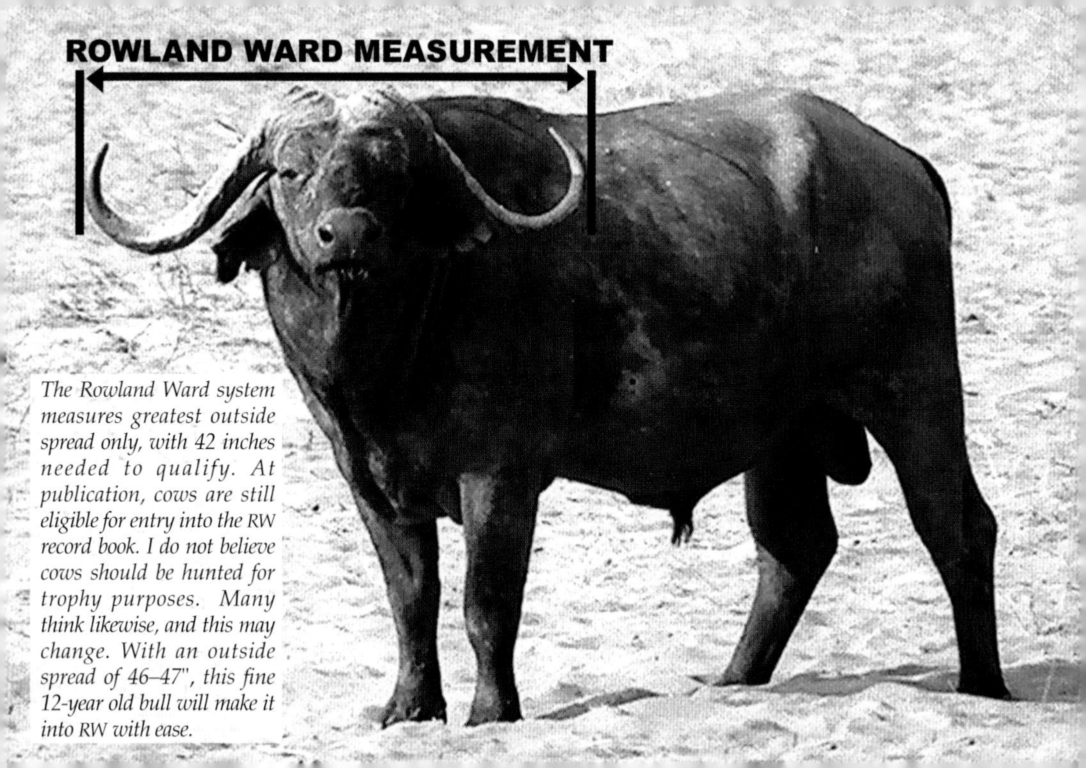


*The Rowland Ward system measures greatest outside spread only, with 42 inches needed to qualify. At publication, cows are still eligible for entry into the* RW *record book. I do not believe cows should be hunted for trophy purposes. Many think likewise, and this may change. With an outside spread of 46–47", this fine 12-year old bull will make it into* RW *with ease.*

*This exceptional young bull was only about 7 years old when photographed. Although too young to fight for the right to breed, he'd score high under both scoring systems. The true sportsman should realize that this bull is still too young to be considered a real trophy, despite the fact that he would most probably rank within the top ten of the SCI record book. His estimated outside horn-spread measurement is at least 48 inches, and maybe as much as 50 inches.*

the current highest-scoring bulls were immature and still held breeding potential when they were collected, can sour the whole process.

There exist two entirely different systems for measuring and recording trophy buffalo. The older system, Rowland Ward's Records of Big Game, originated in Britain in the latter part of the nineteenth century. This is the organization that started it all. Somewhat unfortunately, it has been surpassed in popularity by the more recently formed American organization, Safari Club International and its record-keeping book. Because their respective measuring systems for buffalo differ, each will be dealt with separately.

The Rowland Ward system simply measures the greatest outside spread of a buffalo's horns, in inches to the nearest one-eighth of an inch. Though the inside length of spread, the tip-to-tip length, and the width of the boss are also measured and recorded, all sets that qualify are ranked solely on this single, straight-line measurement. Since 1995 a minimum outside spread of 42 inches has been required for entry into the Rowland Ward record book. The SCI scoring method differs from that of Rowland Ward in that it takes into consideration the tip-to-tip length around the outside of the curl and across the forehead. It also includes in the total score, in inches to the nearest one-eighth, the width of both the left and right boss. A minimum score of 100 is required for SCI record-book entry, and only bulls are eligible.

# Trophy Evaluation
## Chapter 7

A well-mounted set of buffalo horns, requiring considerable physical and emotional effort and no small measure of financial outlay to secure, symbolizes the awesome power, strength, and ruggedness of this remarkable game species. Any ethically collected, solid-bossed buffalo trophy, regardless of its size, should be a conversation piece for a lifetime and evoke memories of the hunt and Africa itself, and therein lies its true value.

To my way of thinking, far too much emphasis is placed today on where a particular trophy will rank "in the book." Whether it even qualifies should not be the be-all and end-all of a successful buffalo hunt—not by a long shot. Those who place "book value" above the true spirit or the ethical fairness of the chase are, in my opinion, missing the very essence of the sport of big-game hunting. The record books have their place, certainly—they are both fascinating and informative references. But they should not be used as a trophy hunter's get-my-name-in-it-at-all-costs Holy Grail!

"I'll shoot it only if it scores well up in the book" is an often heard safari-camp statement. But many PHs dread hearing it because it usually means that the quest for an extra inch or two of total score could well take precedence over what professionals call a "good, hard, and enjoyable hunt." This misplaced value judgment, together with the fact that most of

*The horns on some specimens of* Syncerus cafer cafer *can reach immense size. This bull had a measured outside spread of slightly over 62 inches.*

*Just how much allowance will be determined by the shooting distance and the running speed of the buffalo. Keep your head down, maintain the swing, and follow through with the shot. Remember, too, that solids (recommended for backing up shots) will invariably exit from this angle.*

## SIDE-ON, BACKING UP SHOT

*Side-on backing up shots are a lot more difficult because they require quite a bit more forward allowance.*

## ꞩACK-UP SHOTS

*'ack-up shots invariably ıvolve running buffalo and, ıerefore, moving shots. The ıost common angles are either ıe straight going-away or the uartering-away ones. Solids re usually recommended for hese angles, for the extra enetration needed. Moving, uartering-away angles may equire a small measure of ɔrward allowance. Just how ıuch requires lots of experience ince there are always variables ke speed, angle, and distance ıat will all have an influence n the amount required. A ıoving, quartering-away acking up shot will require a it of forward allowance.*

## LEFT-SIDE, QUARTERING-AWAY SHOT

*A buffalo's rumen lies on the left-hand side. Because of this, never, absolutely never, take an initial shot from this angle. To reach the top of the heart from this position, a shot would have to be placed at the tip of the arrow. This is EXACTLY where the rumen lies! Only backing up shots should be taken from this angle and then with solids so as to be able to penetrate effectively through the ingesta-filled rumen.*

# RIGHT-SIDE, QUARTERING-AWAY SHOT

*More acutely angled, right-hand side, quartering-away shots can also be effective, but they offer no room for shot-placement error. They are not for the inexperienced. Such a shot will penetrate through the liver as well as be effective when it reaches and penetrates into the chest cavity.*

## RIGHT-HAND SIDE, QUARTERING-AWAY SHOT

*Right-hand side, quartering-away shots can, especially if the angle is not too great, be remarkably effective. Because there are other buffalo behind, only an expanding type of bullet from a caliber/cartridge combination that will not exit should be used.*

# QUARTERING TOWARD CHEST SHOT

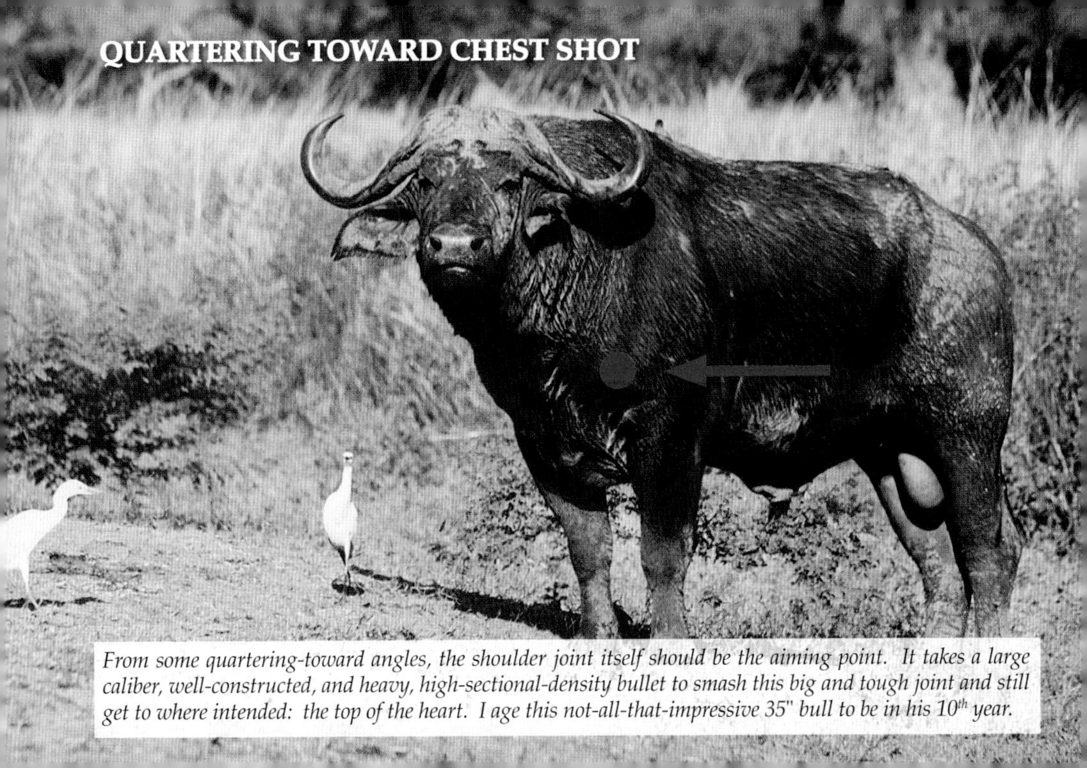

*From some quartering-toward angles, the shoulder joint itself should be the aiming point. It takes a large caliber, well-constructed, and heavy, high-sectional-density bullet to smash this big and tough joint and still get to where intended: the top of the heart. I age this not-all-that-impressive 35" bull to be in his 10th year.*

## QUARTERING FRONTAL CHEST SHOT

*Quartering frontal chest shots are by far the most commonly taken shots at buffalo—and they are effective. From this position, it's all a matter of getting the angles right. The prominent and easily visible shoulder joint will be your reference point. The top of the heart is at this level. This good, solidly bossed herd bull has a 38" spread. This bull has a good solid boss.*

## FULL FRONTAL, HIGH HEART/ LUNG SHOT

*When viewed from the front, the bottom of a buffalo's neck forms a distinct V, with its bottom at shoulder-joint level (arrow). The top of the centrally situated heart is also at this level. This is the position to place a high heart/lung shot.*

*Notice the position of the heart when the front legs are spread far apart. Its top is on the bisecting line of the angle created by the front legs.*

# SHOT PLACEMENT FOR HEART SHOTS WHEN LEGS ARE APART

*When the front legs of a buffalo are spread apart at the time a high heart/lung shot is to be taken, divide the angle created by the leg exactly. The top of the heart will be situated at shoulder-joint level on this bisecting line.*

*The side-on, high heart/lung shot from the ghost view.*

## SIDE-ON, HIGH HEART/LUNG SHOT

*From side-on, come up the centerline of the front leg and place the shot between one-third and certainly no higher than halfway up the body on that line. So placed, the shot will be through the center of the vital triangle—into the top of the heart and the middle of the lungs. I age this fine 40-inch herd bull to be late in his 8th year.*

*Notice how the bottom half of the heart lies beneath the humerus.*

## SIDE-ON, LOW HEART SHOT

*A shot placed as indicated will go through the bottom half of the heart (the ventricles). The shot may well hit the humerus as well. It takes a good bullet to break this tough bone and still penetrate on into the chest cavity.*

*A shot placed as indicated, with a large caliber expanding type bullet, will be in the upper, rearmost part of the lungs. The right type of bullet will kill a buffalo effectively.*

## SIDE-ON, HIGH LUNG SHOT

*The brain is fueled by oxygen, and it is the blood supply to the head that takes oxygen to the brain. With this in mind, there are basically three options for initiating the process to "switch off the brain's fuel supply": the high lung shot, low heart shot, and high-heart/center of the lungs shot.*

*Also known as the "vital triangle" shot, the side-on, high heart/lung shot is by far the most effective from this position. The top of the heart, all the plumbing, and the center of the lungs lie exactly in its center.*

## QUARTERING FRONTAL VIEW OF SHOULDER/ SPINE SHOT

*The shoulder/spine shot is a particularly effective shot whenever it is desirable for the buffalo to drop to the shot. This is where you would place the shot if the bull is facing you at this angle.*

*The shoulder/spinal shot is through the neck of the scapula and then the spinal column that lies directly beneath it. A shot placed here will break the shoulder, break the spine, and sever the spinal cord—and drop a buffalo.*

*The high shoulder/spinal shot is effective and has a good margin for shot-placement error. Placed perfectly, it'll drop a buffalo. There may be a situation when such a reaction will be essential.*

*The neck/spinal shot from the side-on position.*

## NECK/SPINAL SHOT FROM SIDE ON

*This is quite a risky shot, but it does have its place. If placed correctly, this shot will drop a buffalo in its tracks. In some hunting situations, this is a desirable option.*

*Notice how low the spine dips down into the neck area. A shot placed as indicated will drop a buffalo. Be careful in such instances not to place the shot too high, for then it will hit the lower jawbone.*

## SPINAL SHOT: FRONTAL, HEAD UP

*It is sometimes possible to ambush buffalo while they are grazing straight toward you. When they have their heads down, a shot placed into the top of the neck on the centerline is very effective. Be sure to place the shot at shoulder-joint level, just in case it lands off-center. This way it'll still penetrate on into the chest cavity at the top of the heart. This nine-year-old herd bull has a good, 40-plus-inch spread and a fine, almost completely solid boss.*

## FRONTAL BRAIN SHOT: HEAD DOWN

*From the position of this 13-year-old bull's head and because of the close range, a frontal brain shot is really the only shot placement option. When he drops to the shot, run around behind him and shoot him again through the spine and into the boiler room. These insurance shots are necessary.*

# Shot Placement
## Chapter 6

Buffalo have a well-deserved reputation for being extremely dangerous and hard to kill. As I've written many times, make a "perfect shot" and the buffalo will die. No animal, not even a super-tough old buffalo bull, will survive for more than a few minutes with a ruptured aorta or pulmonary artery and collapsed, blood-filled lungs. Neither will it survive a severed spinal column in the neck or shoulder region—it's as simple as that.

Place the initial shot poorly, and you could have a potential problem on your hands, regardless of the caliber you used. In fact, Syncerus's reputation for being apparently bulletproof, ornery, "tougher than nails," and "meaner than sin" is most often the result of poor initial shot placement. I have always been and remain to this day totally convinced of the validity of this statement.

To place the initial shot with absolute precision, it is first necessary to understand the function of the four vital-for-life organs—the brain, the spinal column, the heart, and the lungs. It is also essential to locate their exact position within the huge and muscular buffalo body from any angle. (See chapter 3.) Since life as we know it is controlled by the brain, that is where we'll start in discussing shot placement.

*In some, "up close and personal" buffalo encounters, the frontal brain shot will be the only option. Placed as indicated, the bull should drop to the shot. When it does, put in another shot immediately into the heart/lung area just for insurance.*

*Well-worn and comfortable boots, neutral-colored clothing, a peaked cap, and a thoroughly tested, "Africa-ready" scoped rifle of adequate caliber are essential. Being able to shoot quickly, accurately, and confidently from all field positions is also an essential requirement for hunting buffalo.*

Then there are the right clothes for hunting. It is essential to wear some form of hat or cap, not only for protection from the sun but also for camouflage. I prefer a baseball-type cap in some dark, neutral color. Probably the most important item for your buffalo safari is your boots. Make sure your boots are of good quality and are well worn before you step on a plane for Africa. If your feet hurt and you can't walk, your safari is ruined. A set of gaiters will prevent grass seeds and sand from getting into your socks. Long-sleeved shirts and long pants will prevent scratches and sunburn, but they can be hot. Olive green, tan, and dark khaki are the best colors to wear. Bring a jacket because African nights can be cold.

When packing, don't forget to include shooting sticks, a camera, a flashlight, sunscreen, lip balm, and antimalaria prophylaxis tablets. You don't want to be half a world away and realize the importance of these items to your life and safety.

# Important Accessories
## Chapter 5

A good binocular is essential for a buffalo hunt. A buffalo's eyesight is incredible. It has to be for these animals to be able to detect well-camouflaged lion. To spot a buffalo before he spots you, a good binocular is indispensable. Another important accessory is a small knife or utility tool. A Leatherman or a Swiss Army knife or even just a three-inch lock-blade in a pouch on your belt is useful. Any one of these will be far more practical than a big sheath knife.

Another important accessory is a cartridge belt. Most large-caliber, bolt-action rifles hold at least two but more commonly three or even four cartridges in the magazine, so an additional eight to ten cartridges in a pouch or on your belt will be plenty. Along with a belt, a rifle sling comes in handy. Fitting your rifle with a two-inch-wide sling will spread the weight on your shoulder and make the gun much easier and more comfortable to carry for long periods.

*My recommendations include an adequate rifle/caliber/cartridge combination, a decent binocular (8X30 is ideal), and an 8 to 10 capacity cartridge belt with a sheath knife and GPS on it. A peaked, baseball-type cap, a spare box of ammo (to be carried in daypack), well-worn hunting boots, a decent flashlight, sunscreen, lip balm, and antimalaria prophylaxis tablets are all necessities as well.*

norma
10 CARTRIDGES • 10 CARTOUCHES
AFRICAN PH
505 GIBBS
norma
AFRICAN PH
GARMIN

*First- shot, expanding-type bullets include (from left) the Barnes X-Bullet, Trophy Bonded Bear Claw, Swift A-Frame, Stewart Hi-Performer, Rhino, and Woodleigh Weldcore. All these premium-quality bullets come highly recommended.*

*Always back up with solids. There are many different types from which to choose. Flat-nosed solids tend to penetrate the best. Make sure they shoot to the same point of aim as the chosen expanding bullet.*

*A 500-grain .458 bullet at 2,150 fps is adequate for all PH work. These include (from left) the .458 Winchester Magnum, .458 Lott, .450 Watts, .450 Ackley Magnum, and .458 3″ Express. For double rifles, the .470 NE or the .500 NE are the two best options.*

*The most common client caliber/cartridge recommendations are (from left): 9.3x62mm, 9.3x64mm, .375 Ruger, .375 H&H, .450-400 NE, .404 Jeffery, .416 Rem, .416 Rigby, .458 Win Mag, .458 Lott.*

*For precise first-sh placement when using scope, the whole buffa needs to be in the sig picture for prope orientation. This is wh makes low-powered, 1- or 1.5-5 variables a bett choice over fixed-pow ones. Regardless of calib or cartridge, sight-in t scope on a buffalo rif so that it is "dead on" 100 paces.*

*A typical, modern-day client's rifle will be a turn-bolt of classic lines and proportions with a low-powered, variable scope. It should also be thoroughly tested, Africa ready, and reasonably accurate. A scope will increase buffalo shooting opportunities greatly.*

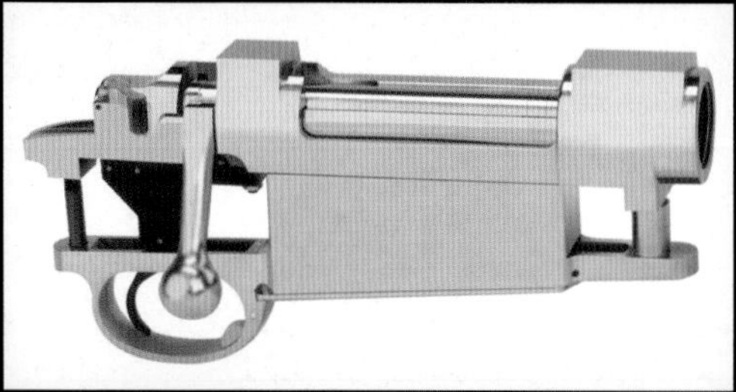

*A Mauser '98-type action, with its positive feed, non-rotating claw extractor is in reality the only action type recommended for serious work on dangerous game.*

*Another option for the big-game rifle is the ghost-ring aperture rear sight. Its advantage is that more of the buffalo will be in view while aiming at your target. For a quartering, frontal-heart shot, sight in for a six o'clock hold as well so that the bullet impacts at the red dot.*

*Even from side-on, an open-express V sight will still cover much of the bull being aimed at. Because of this, the six o'clock hold is the best sighting-in option. This means that at fifty paces the bullet should impact on the red dot for the center of the vital triangle, high-heart shot. This solid bossed twelve-year-old bull has at least a forty-inch spread and is a fine trophy.*

*Fast to align and easy to use, the classic, shallow V, open-express rear sight is the premier choice for most double and PH rifles. Unfortunately, it will cover much of what is being aimed at. To remedy this, sight the target in for a six o'clock hold at fifty paces. The bullet should impact on the red dot for a high heart/ lung shot.*

Conversely, the greater the ballistic performance, the more difficult such combinations will be to shoot both accurately and well. In the end it all boils down to an individual being able to handle confidently and shoot accurately the largest possible caliber/cartridge combination possible. The most common caliber/cartridge recommendations for clients are the 9.3x62mm, 9.3x64mm, .375 Ruger, .375 H&H, .450-400 NE, .404 Jeffery, .416 Remington, .416 Rigby, .458 Winchester Magnum, and .458 Lott.

The Mauser '98 action with its controlled feed and large, nonrotating claw extractor, or one of its modern-day derivatives like the Brno ZKK 602, CZ 550, Ruger M77 MKII, or the pre-'64 Winchester are the ones I recommend as rifles for dangerous game. Safari clients invariably shoot better with scope-sighted rifles. Such a rifle will increase shooting opportunities by as much as 20 percent. The best quality, 1 to 4 power or 1.5 to 5 power variable scope, with a bold and easily visible reticule is the best option for a client's rifle. Double rifles, while a pleasure to both own and use, are not essential for successful buffalo hunting.

## Buffalo: Shot Placement and Trophy Evaluation

The majority of double rifles and most bolt-action PH rifles carry open express V sights. Those with a shallow 140-degree angle are very fast to use, especially if the sight has a vertical gold or platinum line and the foresight is big, bold, and easy to pick out visually. While not as popular as open V sights, ghost ring, rear-aperture sights are just as fast to use when combined with an easily visible foresight bead. Ghost rings and V sights should be sighted in for a six o'clock hold at fifty paces.

Like choosing a suitable rifle, selecting a caliber-and-cartridge combination for it is an important and enjoyable part of any buffalo hunt. For the inexperienced, it can also be extremely confusing because of the many choices available. When it comes to caliber selection and the sporting pursuit of Syncerus, it is vital to remember two important and yet contradictory considerations. First, a smaller-diameter bullet in the right place will be far more effective than a larger, poorly placed one, regardless of their respective ME (muzzle-energy) values. For buffalo, correct and precise first-shot placement is absolutely everything—period. Second, the larger the caliber, the greater will be its visual "hitting punch." Put this way, a large-caliber bullet in the right place will be more effective than a smaller, similarly placed one.

In making a caliber/cartridge selection, there are inevitably going to be trade-offs between ballistic performance and recoil. On the one hand, the more the legal minimum ballistic requirements are exceeded, the more effective the resultant combination will be on buffalo.

# Rifles, Sights, Calibers, Cartridges, and Bullet Selection
## Chapter Four

The most important considerations for any client's rifle are that it be both "shootable" and "Africa-ready." By shootable I mean that its recoil must be manageable for the user. The rifle also needs to be reasonably accurate with the type of bullets to be used and at the desired muzzle velocity. I have stated that a shot in the right place is worth a dozen in the H&H will be just that, while a .460 Weatherby or one of the other monster magnums that show up in safari camps usually is not. Every PH I know would rather have his client put a good .375 bullet through a buffalo's heart than a .458 or larger one in its guts—it's as simple as that. "Africa ready" implies that the rifle has been fired a sufficient number of times to test its functional reliability, construction, and shooting performance thoroughly. A remote African safari camp is not the place to discover that your rifle's stock has developed a crack or that the magazine floor plate keeps dropping open every time a shot is fired!

*Photo opposite page: While a joy to both own and use, a classic double is not essential for successful buffalo hunting. For PH use however, and for wounded buffalo follow-ups, nothing beats a big-bore double like this Holland & Holland .500-450 NE. Notice the big, solid boss on this 10-year-old bull with a 36-inch spread.* (Photo courtesy of Mal McGregor)

*From side-on, the brachial plexus is too small an area to place a shot effectively, and it's one that I don't recommend. From this position, a shot aimed at the center of the vital triangle is always the most effective option.*

## THE BRACHIAL PLEXUS

*This area is located low down on the neck and in front of the shoulder joint. Several anatomical peculiarities are located at this point. All the nerves to the foreleg penetrate through the body from here, in a bundle with the blood vessels of the leg. The front edge of the pleural cavity extends into this area as well. Shots placed here from the quartering frontal position are particularly effective. A buffalo shot from this position often runs away with its right leg apparently paralyzed, which is the result of the nerves to it being severed by the bullet passing through the brachial plexus.*

# THE LIVER

*The liver on a buffalo lies on its right-hand side, just behind the diaphragm. Right-hand-side, quartering-away shots that reach the chest cavity often pass through some part of this internal organ. The liver has a rich blood supply, and it tends to burst when struck with a fully expanded softpoint bullet. Such shots can be particularly debilitating, especially when they penetrate on into the heart/lung area as well. A shot placed as indicated will pass through the liver on its way to the chest cavity.*

## THE KIDNEYS

*The kidneys lie high up in the abdomen, just below the spine and midway between the last rib and the pelvic bone. The kidneys, too, have a rich blood supply, so damaging them with angling-away, backing shots can be particularly debilitating. The position of the left kidney is indicated.*

## THE VITAL TRIANGLE

*Shots placed in the vital triangle usually result in quick kills.*

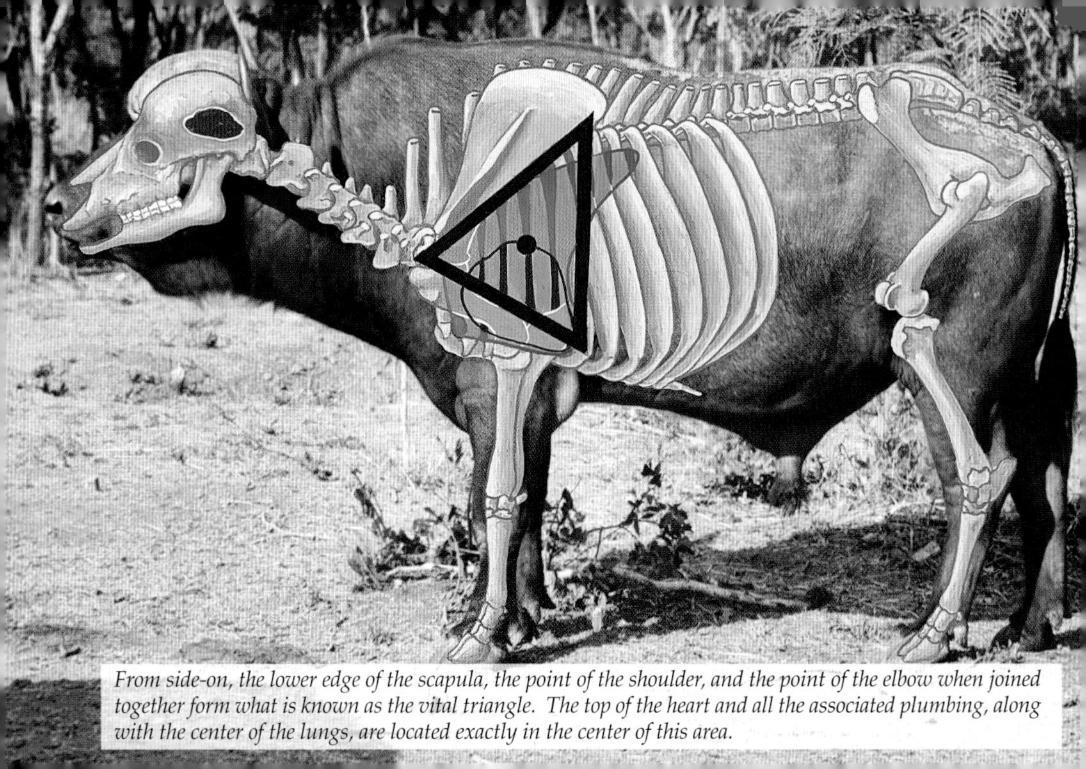

*From side-on, the lower edge of the scapula, the point of the shoulder, and the point of the elbow when joined together form what is known as the vital triangle. The top of the heart and all the associated plumbing, along with the center of the lungs, are located exactly in the center of this area.*

## TRAMPOLINE EFFECT

*A buffalo's skin in the frontal chest area is nearly an inch thick. It is also loose and supple. This protects the front of the chest when buffalo crash through the thickest cover. This thick skin has "give," which can absorb and dissipate a bullet's kinetic energy. The loose and supple frontal chest skin causes the phenomenon known as the trampoline effect.*

# THE RUMEN

*A buffalo's rumen is voluminous. It lies on the left-hand side of the abdominal cavity and fills the majority of it. Because of its internal position in the body, all left-hand-side, quartering-away shots will need to pass through the rumen if they are to reach the chest cavity. Rumen content is puttylike and can seriously affect a bullet's terminal performance.*

# THE LUNGS

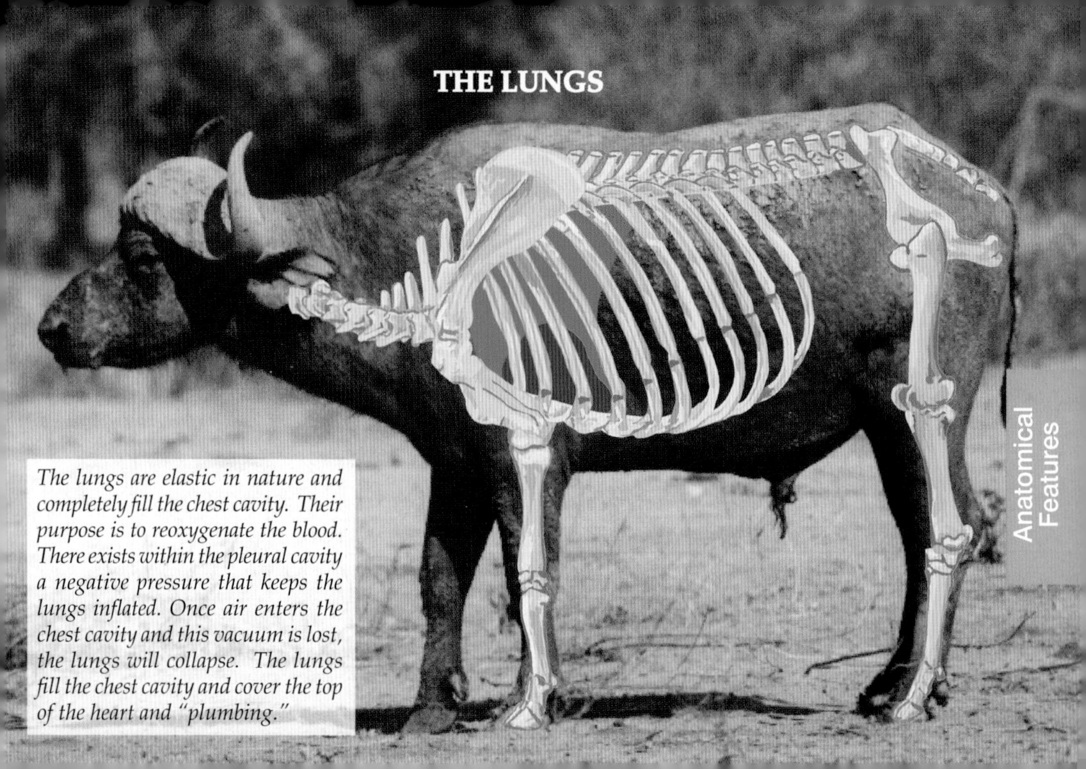

*The lungs are elastic in nature and completely fill the chest cavity. Their purpose is to reoxygenate the blood. There exists within the pleural cavity a negative pressure that keeps the lungs inflated. Once air enters the chest cavity and this vacuum is lost, the lungs will collapse. The lungs fill the chest cavity and cover the top of the heart and "plumbing."*

# THE HEART

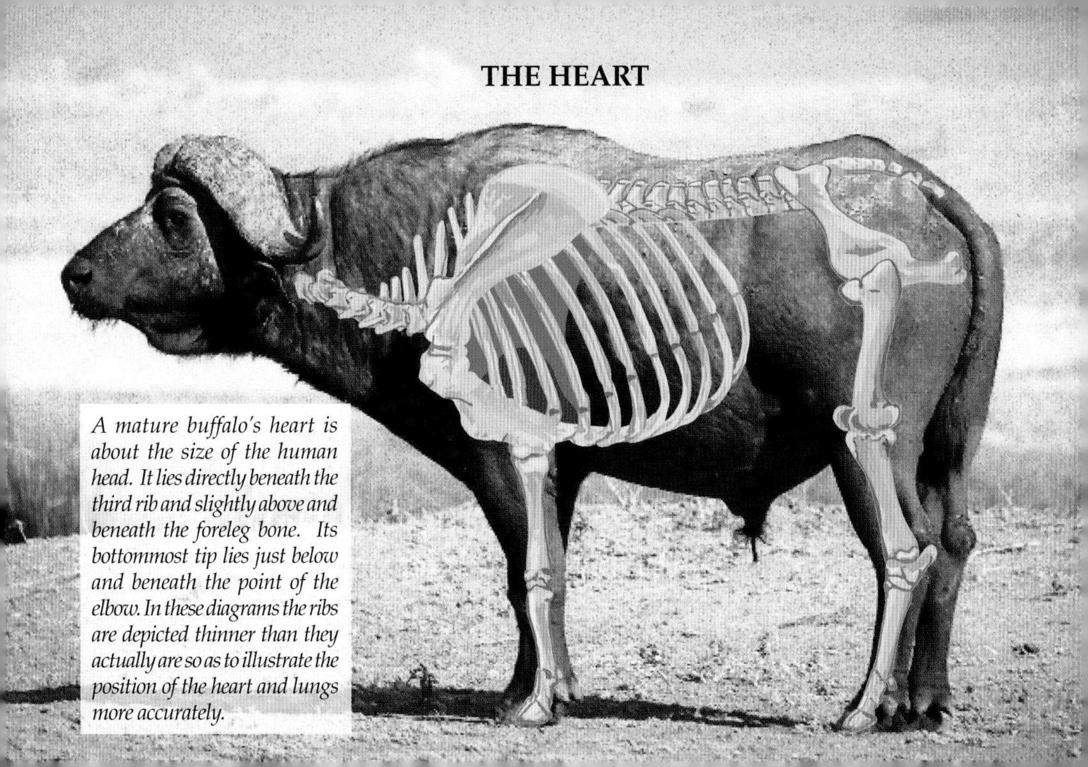

*A mature buffalo's heart is about the size of the human head. It lies directly beneath the third rib and slightly above and beneath the foreleg bone. Its bottommost tip lies just below and beneath the point of the elbow. In these diagrams the ribs are depicted thinner than they actually are so as to illustrate the position of the heart and lungs more accurately.*

# THE SPINAL COLUMN

*From just behind the shoulder, the spinal column dips downward steeply in the shoulder region. It reaches its lowest level just in front of the point of the shoulder. The spine is almost exactly in the middle of the neck where the neck joins the body. From the front, a buffalo's rib cage is shaped just like the bow of a ship. Notice how low the spinal column dips in the shoulder region as well as the position of the heart.*

## THE RIBS

*A buffalo's rib cage is shaped like the bow of a ship, which is important to know for frontal chest shots. The rear-most ribs are heavily curved while those that lie farther forward are less so. Because they overlap, the ribs form a smooth outer layer, and only between the first four is there a small intercostal space. The heart lies beneath the third rib. Side-on shots invariably hit a rib as they penetrate the chest cavity.*

# THE BRAIN

*When a buffalo looks at you with that typical, nose-uplifted "I hate you" stare, the brain is at the same level as the top half of the nostrils. The bull doing the staring is 7 years old and still soft bossed.*

# THE BRAIN

*A buffalo's brain is small in comparison to the size of its head. Its position within the skull is between the eyes and the ear holes. From the side the brain is well protected by the downward sweep of the horns, while the boss protects the brain from above.*

*Viewed from above, the heart, lungs, rumen, liver, and spleen are shown. Note the position of the rumen, which fills most of the left-hand side of the abdominal cavity. Quartering-away shots from the left-hand side are never a good option because of the position of the rumen. The liver lies on the right-hand side and just behind the diaphragm.*

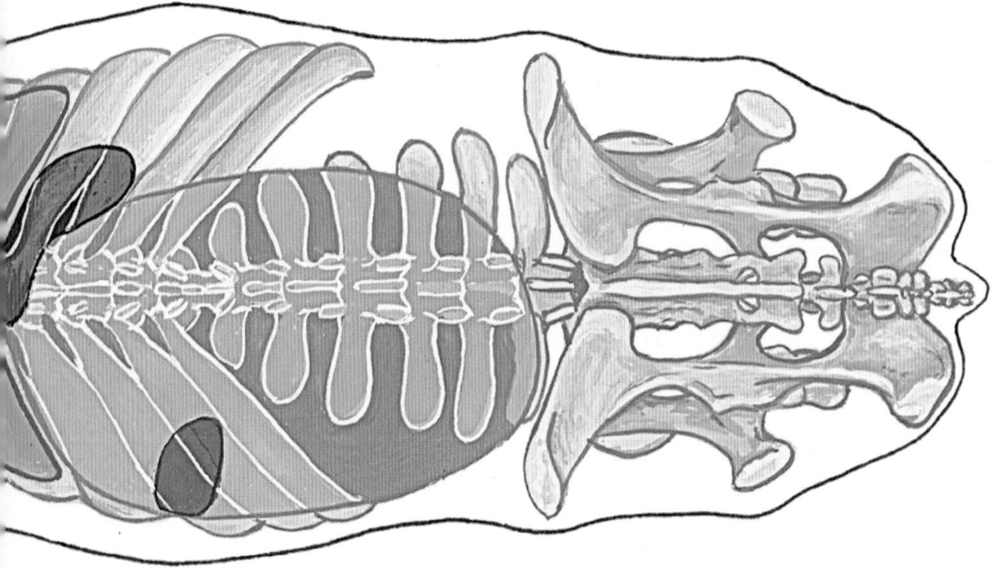

# INTERNAL ORGANS

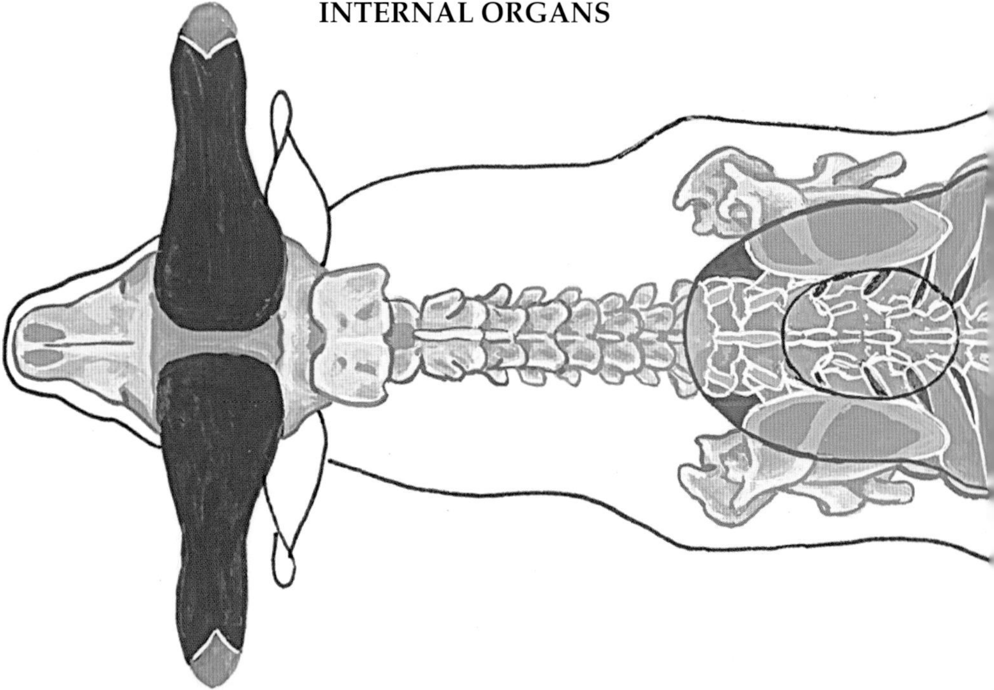

## INTERNAL ORGANS, RIGHT SIDE

*Most importantly, the liver is situated on the right-hand side. Also indicated are the brain, the heart, lungs, right kidney, and intestines.*

*The same bull viewed from his right-hand side.*

## INTERNAL ORGANS, LEFT SIDE

*Viewed from the left, the internal positions of the heart, lungs, rumen, spleen, and left kidney can be seen.*

*There is a difference to what a buffalo looks like internally when viewed from either the left- or right-hand side. This is the left-hand view of a mature bull buffalo.*

in the exact center of this area; consequently, this area is the most vulnerable place on a buffalo.

The liver lies on a bull's right-hand side just behind the diaphragm. The liver is encapsulated and brittle and tends to burst when struck with a fully expanded softpoint bullet. The kidneys are situated well to the rear and high up in the abdomen. They lie just below the spine and midway between the last rib and the pelvic bone.

The brachial plexus is an approximately four-square-inch area located low on the base of the neck, just in front of the shoulder joint. All the nerves to the foreleg branch off the spinal cord and penetrate through the body wall at this point. A well-constructed expanding bullet passing through this area on its way into the chest cavity will be as effective as a well-placed one into the vital triangle.

## Buffalo: Shot Placement and Trophy Evaluation

The heart on a mature buffalo is big, about the size of a human head. It lies directly beneath the third rib and slightly above and beneath the humerus or foreleg bone. Its bottom tip is just below and beneath the point of the elbow.

The lungs are elastic in nature and extend only as far forward as the point of the shoulder and the first rib, although the pleural cavity extends an additional few inches farther forward in front of the first rib.

The rumen, which has the capacity of a forty-four-gallon fuel drum, is the large, four-chambered stomach of the buffalo. The rumen lies on the left-hand side of the abdominal cavity and fills the majority of it.

The frontal chest skin, like all skin on a buffalo, is incredibly tough. Because it is loose and supple, the chest skin also has "give," which enables it to be pushed inward. It absorbs and dissipates a bullet's kinetic energy and will cause a softpoint bullet to set up* and mushroom, a phenomenon known as the trampoline effect.

The vital triangle is where the line of the lower edge of the scapula, the point of the shoulder, and the point of the elbow when joined together form a triangular-shaped area. The top of the heart, the center of the lungs, and all the "plumbing" are located

*Set up is the process whereby an expanding type of bullet (a softpoint) opens up and in so doing takes on the shape of a mushroom.

# Important Anatomical Features
## Chapter Three

Identifying the internal features of a buffalo depends on whether you are viewing one from its left- or right-hand side. The rumen or paunch occupies most of the abdominal cavity's left-hand side, while the liver lies well forward and more to the right. The next five photos illustrate this point. The other important anatomical features will be dealt with pictorially throughout this chapter. These are the boss (left), brain, ribs, rib cage, spinal column, heart, lungs, rumen, frontal chest skin, vital triangle, liver, kidneys, and brachial plexus.

The boss on a mature bull is solid. It is there to protect the top of the head and brain.

The brain on a buffalo is small in comparison to the size of its head. When a buffalo looks at you with its nose uplifted, the brain will be positioned at or just above the nostril level.

The ribs on a buffalo are comprised of extremely hard bone, are thick and broad, and their edges overlap to form what is essentially a bony shield. Only between the first four ribs is there a narrow intercostal space.

The rib cage is shaped much like the bow of a ship. The rearmost ribs are heavily curved while those farther forward are less so. Because they overlap, the ribs form a smooth outer layer.

The spinal column, from just behind the shoulder, dips downward steeply in the shoulder region, and reaches its lowest level just in front of the point of the shoulder.

## THE BOSS

*On mature, 10-year-old (and older) buffalo bulls, a solid boss will cover the top of the head. Its function is to protect the brain during head-butting, test-of-strength contests. There will always be a small, softer area of skin between the two halves of even the largest boss.*

*Horn deformities can confuse sex determination. In some conditions, this mature but masculine-looking cow could easily be mistaken for a wide-spreading, high-scoring bull.*

*Cows can attain exceptional horn spread; this one must be close to 50 inches.*

*Mature, 10-year-old (and older) bulls will have a completely solid boss. The boss on this twelve-year-old bull is exceptional. Combined with his forty-inch spread, this is a fine trophy. Hairless patches on a mature bull's face are due to mite infestations.*

*Immature buffalo bulls do not have a well-defined boss; instead, the forehead will be light gray and covered with a few coarse black hairs. The horn tips are usually sharp and above the level of the boss. This bull is approximately 6 years old.*

*Mature buffalo bulls in good body condition are massive and heavily muscled. A well-formed solid boss and easily visible penis sheath clearly show the sex of this 9-year-old buffalo bull. The spread is at least 40 inches.*

*Even on mature cows the forehead will still be covered with sparse hair, and the horns will appear to grow out the side of the head.*

*Cows, too, can have backward-sweeping horns similar to those of younger bulls. The lack of a boss and a penis sheath clearly indicates that this is a mature cow.*

*Mature cows can easily attain the body size and shape of a bull. They do not, however, develop the heavy muscling associated with masculinity. The lack of a boss and a penis sheath clearly indicates that this is a big-bodied cow.* (Photo C. Bone)

*At a glance this young, 4-year-old bull could easily be mistaken for a cow. His penis sheath is the most distinguishable feature, which clearly indicates he is not a cow. Notice his soft boss and sharp, rearward-pointing horn tips.*

*When buffalo are out in the open, sex determination is easier. Take every opportunity to practice differentiating between the sexes at such times. From the left you will see a mature cow; an immature, soft-bossed, 6-year-old bull; another mature cow with her head raised; another soft-bossed, 6-year-old bull; and a younger cow on the right.*

difficult to see, so do not rely on being able to use this anatomical feature to determine the sex of a buffalo. Cows have thin, slender, and feminine necks. Their forequarters are neither muscular nor well developed. No cow has a boss; instead, their horns just appear to grow out of the side of the head. The forehead is usually white-gray in color and sparsely covered with coarse black hairs. Despite this, horn spread of some cows can still be impressive. For various reasons, both cows and bulls will sometimes rub their foreheads against termite mounds. When this happens, a cow's mud-covered forehead can easily be mistaken for a bull's solid boss, especially if the horns are wide-spreading and if visibility is restricted. Be careful of this, and always remember to check the belly-line before shooting.

## Buffalo: Shot Placement and Trophy Evaluation

The only way to be absolutely sure of any buffalo's sex, regardless of its age, is to look at its ventral bodyline. All bulls have a well-developed and hairy, penis sheath. It is distinctly visible and hangs down almost vertically. Some cows may have a small and rounded umbilical button in the same area, but if present it is usually smooth and hairless.

Mature buffalo bulls are the biggest in body size. Due to their male characteristics, they have heavily muscled shoulders and massively thick necks. These together with a solid boss and possibly blunt, worn-down horn tips are their most characteristic physical features. It is unusual for the horn tips of old bulls to stick high above the level of the boss. Fully mature bulls usually have hairless patches on their hides and scaly white-gray areas on their faces or around their eyes. As mentioned above, the penis sheath is usually well developed and distinctly visible.

Immature buffalo bulls are generally smaller in overall body size as a result of their lack of heavy muscling, especially in the shoulder and neck region. The most noticeable feature with such bulls, however, is the boss. It will be soft, light gray in color, and sometimes still covered with a few coarse black hairs. The horn tips on immature bulls will be sharp and above the level of the boss. The tips may also point to the rear. It is unusual for immature bulls to have hairless patches on their faces.

Buffalo cows vary tremendously in body size and, to some extent, body shape as well. This is a result of their age, nutritional status, and hormonal balance. The udder is small and

# Sex Determination
## Chapter Two

Shooting the wrong sex of buffalo is one of the most embarrassing situations a hunter can experience. And it happens, more often than many will admit. The reason lies in the fact that buffalo are by their nature cautious and suspiciously wary creatures. They are also gregarious herd animals that continuously intermingle in proximity with one another. During the heat of the day they favor thick bush situations or areas of long grass that offer limited visibility for the hunter. This, together with their uniform, gray-black color, enables them to blend with the shadows most effectively.

When buffalo are out in the open, sex determination is easier, and it's the wise hunter who takes every opportunity to practice differentiating between the sexes. There are two problem areas most commonly experienced when trying to differentiate the sexes. The first one requires the hunter to be able to recognize the difference between young, immature, not-all-that-well-muscled bulls and mature cows. The second problem results from the fact that some large-framed cows—especially when not lactating—in peak condition or hormonally disturbed can easily be as heavy and have a body shape similar to that of a mature bull.

*Photo opposite page: For safety, buffalo prefer to stay bunched up and in proximity to one another whenever they are in a herd. This can make sex determination difficult.*

*At least eight hours out of every twenty-four will be spent ruminating. This activity is usually carried out while lying down in the sternal recumbency position. This mature, 38-inch-spread bull is at least ten years old. His completely solid boss, his obviously worn-down horn tips, and the hairless areas on his face make this estimate accurate.*

*Buffalo are gregarious herd animals. The bull looking at the camera is eight years old. His boss is just about solid and his horn tips, while still sharp, are pointing slightly to the back. This is what determines his age quite accurately.*

bulls make up about eight percent of a herd. A herd bull's life is not easy. Being constantly on guard, always grazing at the back of the herd on already trampled grass, and having to fight off challengers continually takes its toll on the bull's body condition and strength. When these factors decline, breeding bulls will leave their herds to join up with bachelor bull groups. This period of R&R enables them to regain their weight and strength.

They rejoin the herds when they are once again strong enough to fight for dominance. It is for this reason bulls of breeding age can occur in bachelor herds, and that is why it is so important to be able to judge the age of a bull accurately. Sometime late in their tenth or eleventh year, this type of bull will usually be permanently replaced by younger, stronger, and fitter eight-year-old breeding bulls. These post-breeding bulls are referred to as *dagga* boys, and these are the ones that should be targeted by the trophy hunter.

position. Buffalo rest up in deep shade during the heat of the day and again at some stage during the night—usually in an open area. This is when they ruminate most actively.

Early mornings and late afternoon are their most active grazing periods. They will usually spread out and feed into or across the prevailing wind while doing so, moving in a slow and meandering zigzag sort of pattern. They do this so that their refined sense of smell can warn them of any danger up ahead. Bulls usually graze toward the back part of the herd because this is the most vulnerable area for attacks by lion.

Buffalo are a long-lived, slow-maturing species. Sexual maturity depends on their growth rate and is attained when they reach 66 percent of their mature body mass. Environmental factors, especially rainfall, have the greatest influence on buffalo growth rate.

Cows reach sexual maturity at three to four years of age. Their gestation period is approximately eleven months. Calving usually takes place during the latter part of the summer rainy season when nutritional levels and body condition are optimal. A cow's first calf will be born when she is somewhere between four and five years old. Cows usually reproduce every second year, and most cows have between two and four calves in their lifetime. Life expectancy of cows is about fifteen years.

Bulls also reach sexual maturity around three to four years of age, but it is not until they are in their eighth year that they attain the body size, strength, and degree of boss hardness that enables them to compete physically for dominance and, therefore, breeding favors. Breeding

# *Syncerus cafer cafer*—The Basic Facts
## Chapter 1

Buffalo are bovines. They are gregarious herd animals. Herd size can vary from only a few to many hundreds. There are approximately 500,000 southern buffalo in southern and eastern Africa, and about 6,000 are sport hunted annually for trophy purposes.

Buffalo are bulk-grazing animals. Their large hoofs and substantial numbers are important because these factors contribute to trampling down tall, unproductive grass, the regrowth of which makes the veld better for those species that need selective grazing. The basic survival needs of buffalo are simply adequate grass, water, and shade. Buffalo dung is moist and sloppy, which indicates they are poor conservers of water. Because of this they need to drink at least once in every thirty-six hours. Most buffalo drink daily, however, and sometimes even twice daily, especially when it is really hot. In safari areas, buffalo usually drink in the evening or at night. They feed their way both to and from water.

The bovine digestive system requires that at least eight hours in every twenty-four be spent ruminating. This buffalo usually do while lying down in the sternal recumbency*

*Sternal recumbency takes place when the animal lies down on its ventral thoracic and abdominal walls, usually with the legs tucked underneath the body. It is also sometimes called dorsal recumbency.

Nat.

# INTRODUCTION

*Syncerus cafer cafer,* the southern buffalo, is without a doubt, Africa's most formidable game animal. From the sport-hunting perspective, they are responsible for more fatalities than any other dangerous species found on the Dark Continent. Dangerous they may be, but immortal they certainly are not. While insurance or backing shots are still essential, a single, well-placed bullet from an adequate caliber is all it takes to bring down one of these formidable black bovines. The secret to accomplishing this lies in getting in nice and close and placing the initial shot in exactly the right place. Many have accomplished this in the past, and it is my hope that this booklet will assist more to do so in the future.

It is also my hope that this booklet will bring about a better understanding of how to age a buffalo accurately. Too many young bulls of breeding age or potential are shot as "trophies" simply because they will score well in the record books. For the long-term benefit and well being of the species, this is wrong. Sport or trophy hunters need to redefine what constitutes a good buffalo trophy, and it is my contention that it should not be a young bull with a soft boss and long, sharp, and backward pointing horn tips.

The real trophies are the old *dagga* boys. These buffalo are eleven years old or older and are past breeding age, which is the important consideration here. No buffalo gets to become a *dagga* boy without being tough, smart, and clever. The sporting pursuit of these old gentlemen is what buffalo hunting is all about. They are the "real" trophies, despite what the record books my say. I hope you agree.

# ACKNOWLEDGMENTS

Without Catherine's, my wife, photographs, this book would be meaningless. For them and the thirty interesting years we have spent together in Africa, my most grateful thanks.

Our daughter Samantha generated images and made photo enhancements on her computer, and for that I am also grateful, for these images are also a large part of this work. So are Cathy Nel's detailed anatomy diagrams. To you both, my appreciation and thanks. Natalie's (our second daughter) buffalo sketches and painting also appear in this work. To her as well, my appreciation and thanks.

# TABLE OF CONTENTS

For a complete description of all Perfect Shot products, go to **Safaripress.com**.

# DEDICATION

*To our respective parents*

*Robbie & Loraine*

*Neville & Margot*

*In appreciation for all the opportunities you have given us in life.*

Kevin & Catherine